AF428597

MY GENERATION

**What group were you born in?
What do the generations represent?**

Kevin B DiBacco

No part of this book may be reproduced in any form without written permission from the publisher or author, except as allowed by U.S. copyright law.

DISCLAIMER

**Kevin's Remarkable Journey of
Strength and Resilience**

Kevin's lifelong passion for
powerlifting and fitness has been
nothing short of remarkable. Though
the journey has been marked by
numerous injuries and surgeries,
Kevin has persevered with

unwavering determination. His medical history reads like an orthopedic textbook: 6 knee operations, 2 major back surgeries, 2 hip replacements, brain surgery and brain radiation. But no amount of adversity could extinguish Kevin's inner fire and drive.

At the age of 62, Kevin undertook a monumental fitness journey to shed 60 pounds, proving that age is just a number. His passion for health and fitness remained undimmed by the passing years. Through all the ups and downs, Kevin persevered with an indomitable spirit.

He now aims to share his hard-won wisdom with others who are facing adversity. Drawing from his experiences, Kevin developed "ISO

QUICK STRENGTH," a program designed to help people rebound after setbacks. He recognized that overcoming difficulties requires both physical and mental strength.

Kevin spreads his message of resilience and determination through a blog, books, and his personal mantra: "Those who quit will always fail." These simple yet powerful words encapsulate his incredible journey. After 37 remarkable years as a filmmaker, and 5 worldwide film distribution deals, Kevin now uses his gifts as a published author to share inspirational stories. With his latest release, "The Gabardine Gang," and his three best-selling books in 2024, "HYSOMETRICS," "Indie Filmmaking in the REAL WORLD," and "Hold the Power,"

Kevin continues to inspire and motivate readers around the world.

Earning the moniker "Life Warrior," Kevin stands as a shining example of the human capacity to overcome any adversity. His unwillingness to ever quit or back down, no matter the obstacles faced, is a testament to the motto he lives by: "A Life Warrior is willing to do whatever it takes to overcome life's challenges."

Kevin's journey has not been linear or easy. But through perseverance, inner strength, and an unbreakable warrior spirit, he has overcome obstacles that would have defeated lesser men. Though battered and bruised, Kevin stands tall as a shining example of human potential. His story is one of courage, resilience, and the power of embracing life's challenges with an open heart.

Kevin has used the visualization technique countless times. Many of his film projects were shot in his head long before filming began. During that time, Kevin has used visualization to produce Movies, TV shows, Documentaries, Music Videos and even as an Author. Before his career in film, he was a successful powerlifter that used 'visualization' and 'positive thinking' techniques when competing.

To this day, visualization is a tool Kevin uses regularly. Kevin has a motto that he lives by, "If you can see it, you can do it". After a remarkable 37-year career as a filmmaker and video producer, Kevin now wields the mighty pen to craft captivating stories in the form of books.

INTRODUCTION

In the tapestry of human history, each generation weaves its own unique thread, contributing to the rich and complex fabric of our shared experience. From the resilient Silent Generation to the tech-savvy Generation Alpha, every cohort has left an indelible mark on society, shaping our world in ways both subtle and profound. "My Generation" invites readers on a fascinating journey through time, exploring the distinct characteristics, values, and contributions of each generation that has shaped our recent history and continues to influence our future.

As we embark on this exploration, we are reminded that the concept of generational cohorts is more than just a sociological curiosity—it's a powerful lens through which we can understand the evolving nature of our society, our values, and our aspirations. Each generation is molded by the unique circumstances of its time, from world-changing events and technological revolutions to shifting social norms and economic realities.

By understanding these generational differences, we gain invaluable insights into the forces that have shaped our world and the challenges and opportunities that lie ahead.

Our journey begins with the Silent Generation, born between 1928 and 1945. Growing up in the shadow of the Great Depression and World War II, this cohort learned the values of hard work, frugality, and resilience. Despite their name, the Silent Generation has been anything but quiet in their contributions to society. Their experiences fostered a deep sense of duty and commitment to community, laying the groundwork for many of the institutions and values we hold dear today.

Next, we encounter the Baby Boomers, the post-war generation born between 1946 and 1964. As the largest generational cohort in history at the time, Baby Boomers have wielded significant influence over culture, politics, and the economy. Known for their idealism and drive for personal fulfillment, this generation spearheaded social movements that reshaped society, from civil rights to environmentalism. Their legacy continues to reverberate through our cultural and political landscapes.

Generation X, born between 1965 and 1980, emerged as a bridge between the analog and digital worlds. Often overlooked between the larger Boomer and Millennial cohorts, Gen Xers have quietly revolutionized the workplace with their entrepreneurial spirit and emphasis on work-life balance. Their adaptability in the face of rapid technological change has been crucial in ushering in the digital age we now inhabit.

The Millennial generation, born between 1981 and 1996, came of age alongside the internet and social media. As digital natives, they have leveraged technology to connect globally and advocate for social change. Millennials have challenged traditional notions of career, lifestyle, and success, prioritizing experiences and personal growth over material wealth. Their influence has reshaped industries and sparked conversations about sustainability, inclusivity, and mental health.

Generation Z, born between 1997 and 2012, represents the first truly global generation. Growing up in a hyper-connected world, Gen Z is known for its diversity, social consciousness, and digital fluency. This generation is at the forefront of discussions on climate change, social justice, and technological ethics, wielding their collective voice to demand a more equitable and sustainable future.

Finally, we look to the future with Generation Alpha, born from 2013 onwards. As the children of Millennials, this generation is growing up in a world where artificial intelligence, virtual reality, and climate change are everyday realities. While it's too early to define their characteristics fully, early indications suggest that Generation Alpha will be the most technologically integrated, globally minded, and change-oriented generation yet.

As we delve into each of these generations, "My Generation" offers more than just a chronicle of demographic shifts. It provides a nuanced exploration of how each cohort has navigated the challenges of its time, contributing to the ongoing story of human progress. From the Silent Generation's emphasis on civic duty to Generation Alpha's innate understanding of global interconnectedness, each generation offers valuable lessons and perspectives that can guide us in addressing the complex challenges of our time.

One of the key themes that emerges from this generational study is the power of resilience and adaptability. Each generation has faced its own set of challenges, from economic depressions and world wars to technological disruptions and environmental crises. Yet, time and again, we see how human ingenuity and determination have allowed us to overcome these obstacles and emerge stronger. This resilience is a testament to the human spirit and a source of hope as we face the uncertainties of the future.

Another crucial insight is the cyclical nature of generational values and priorities. While each generation is unique, we often see patterns emerge across generations. For instance, the civic mindedness of the Silent Generation finds echoes in the social consciousness of Generation Z. The countercultural movements of the Boomers resonate with the disruptive innovations of Millennials. By recognizing these patterns, we can better anticipate future trends and prepare for the challenges and opportunities that lie ahead.

The book also highlights the importance of intergenerational dialogue and collaboration. In our rapidly changing world, the perspectives and skills of all generations are needed to address complex global challenges. The wisdom and experience of older generations, combined with the technological savvy and fresh perspectives of younger cohorts, can create powerful synergies. By fostering understanding and cooperation across generational lines, we can harness our collective strengths to build a more inclusive and sustainable future.

As we look to the future, the study of generations offers valuable insights into emerging trends and potential challenges. For instance, the digital native status of younger generations points to a future where technology will be even more deeply integrated into all aspects of life. This presents opportunities for innovation and efficiency, but also raises important questions about privacy, digital ethics, and the nature of human interaction.

The increasing emphasis on social justice and environmental sustainability across recent generations suggests that these issues will continue to be at the forefront of social and political discourse.

Businesses, governments, and institutions will need to adapt to meet the expectations of consumers and citizens who prioritize ethical practices and sustainable solutions.

The changing nature of work, as exemplified by the gig economy embraced by many Millennials and Gen Zers, indicates a future where traditional career paths may become less relevant. Education systems and workplace policies will need to evolve to support more flexible,

project-based work arrangements
and lifelong learning.

The global mindset of younger
generations, facilitated by digital
connectivity, points to a future where
national boundaries may become
less significant in the face of global
challenges and opportunities. This
could lead to new forms of
international cooperation, but also
presents challenges in terms of
governance and cultural
preservation.

As we navigate these future trends,
the lessons from past generations
become invaluable. The adaptability
of Generation X in the face of
technological change, the civic

engagement of Baby Boomers, and the resilience of the Silent Generation all offer strategies for thriving in times of transformation.

"My Generation" serves as both a celebration of our generational diversity and a call to action. By understanding our shared history and the unique contributions of each generation, we are better equipped to face the challenges of the present and build a brighter future. The book reminds us that while each generation is shaped by its circumstances, we all have the power to shape the world we inhabit.

As you delve into the pages of this book, you'll discover fascinating insights into the events, technologies, and cultural shifts that have defined each generation. You'll explore how the Silent Generation's experiences during the Great Depression influenced their approach to finances and security.

You'll learn about the Baby Boomers' role in shaping modern consumer culture and their impact on social institutions.

You'll gain a deeper understanding of how Generation X's skepticism and independence paved the way for entrepreneurial innovation.

The book also sheds light on the Millennial generation's quest for purpose and meaning in work and life, and how this has led to significant shifts in workplace culture and societal expectations.

You'll explore how Generation Z's digital nativity and global awareness are reshaping education, activism, and communication. And you'll get a glimpse into the potential future shaped by Generation Alpha, as they grow up in a world of artificial intelligence, climate change, and unprecedented global connectivity.

Throughout the book, you'll find compelling stories and data that illustrate how each generation has navigated its unique challenges and opportunities. You'll see how historical events, technological advancements, and social movements have shaped generational characteristics and values. And you'll discover surprising connections and continuities across generations, challenging some of the stereotypes and assumptions we often hold about generational differences.

But "My Generation" is more than just a historical account or sociological study. It's an invitation to reflect on our own place within this generational tapestry. As you read, you'll be encouraged to consider how your own experiences and values have been shaped by your generational context, and how you might bridge generational divides in your personal and professional life.

The book also offers practical insights for leaders, educators, marketers, and policymakers on how to effectively engage with different generations. Whether you're trying to build a multi-generational workforce, design products and services for diverse age groups, or create policies that address the needs of all generations, you'll find valuable guidance and strategies.

As we conclude this introduction, it's important to remember that while generational studies offer powerful insights, they are not deterministic. Within each generation, there is a vast diversity of experiences, perspectives, and values. The goal of "My Generation" is not to pigeonhole individuals into rigid generational categories, but to provide a framework for understanding broad social trends and fostering intergenerational understanding and cooperation.

In the pages that follow, you'll embark on a journey through time, exploring the unique contributions and challenges of each generation.

You'll gain a deeper appreciation for the complex interplay of historical events, technological advancements, and social dynamics that shape generational identities.

And most importantly, you'll be inspired to consider how we can harness the strengths of all generations to create a more inclusive, sustainable, and prosperous future for all.

As we stand at the crossroads of multiple global challenges – from climate change and technological disruption to social inequality and political polarization – the insights offered by this generational exploration become more crucial than ever.

By understanding where we've come from and how each generation has contributed to our collective journey, we are better equipped to chart a course towards a brighter future.

So, let us begin this exploration of "My Generation" with open minds and curious hearts, ready to discover the rich tapestry of human experience that connects us across the generations.

Chapter 1:

What the different Generations tell us?

What the different Generations tell us? This book "My Generation" is a fascinating book that sheds light on the unique characteristics, values, and perspectives of each generation. Through studying the various generations, we can gain valuable insights into how societal influences, technological advancements, and cultural shifts have shaped their beliefs and behaviors.

The Silent Generation, born between the mid-1920s and early 1940s, grew up during times of economic hardship and war. As a result, they tend to value hard work, discipline, and loyalty. Their experiences have instilled in them a sense of resilience and a strong work ethic.

Baby Boomers, born between the mid-1940s and mid-1960s, are known for their idealism and desire for social change. They came of age during a time of significant cultural upheaval, and their values reflect a desire for equality, individualism, and personal fulfillment.

Generation X, born between the mid-1960s and early 1980s, grew up in a time of economic uncertainty and rapid technological advancement. As a result, they tend to be independent, entrepreneurial, and adaptable. They value work-life balance and are known for their skepticism and pragmatism.

Millennials, born between the early 1980s and mid-1990s, are the first generation to come of age in the digital era. They are characterized by their comfort with technology, optimism, and desire for meaningful work. Millennials value diversity, inclusion, and social responsibility.

Generation Z, born from the mid-1990s to the early 2010s, are true digital natives who have grown up in a world of constant connectivity and instant access to information. They are known for their entrepreneurial spirit, creativity, and commitment to making a positive impact on the world.

By understanding the values, experiences, and perspectives of each generation, we can better appreciate the diversity and richness that each brings to our society. What the different Generations tell us? serves as a reminder that each generation has a unique story to tell and a valuable contribution to make.

Chapter 2:

The Greatest Generation or G.I. Generation: Born 1901-1927

Born between 1901 and 1927, this remarkable generation has been hailed as one of the greatest in history. They endured the Great Depression, fought in World War II, and then went on to rebuild their nations and create a better future for the generations that followed.

The men and women of this generation are known for their resilience, their work ethic, and their sense of duty. They understood the

value of hard work, sacrifice, and
community.

They believed in standing up for
what is right and fighting for freedom
and democracy. Education was
highly valued by the Greatest
Generation. Many of them did not
have the opportunity to receive a
formal education due to the
economic challenges of the time, but
they understood the importance of
learning and self-improvement.

They instilled in their children the
belief that education was the key to
a better life and a brighter future.
Despite facing hardships and
adversity, the Greatest Generation
showed incredible determination and
perseverance.

They worked tirelessly to provide for their families, to rebuild their countries, and to create a more prosperous world for future generations. Today, we can learn valuable lessons from the Greatest Generation.

Their strong sense of community, their commitment to hard work, and their unwavering belief in the power of education are all qualities that we can strive to emulate. By honoring their legacy and embodying their values, we can continue to build a better world for ourselves and for generations to come.

The Greatest Generation

Known as the G.I. Generation includes individuals born between 1901 and 1927.

This generation is known for their remarkable resilience, strong work ethic, and unwavering dedication to their country. Here are some of the key characteristics that make the Greatest Generation special and different:

1. Shaped by the Great Depression and World War II:

The Greatest Generation came of age during the Great Depression and World War II, two of the most significant events of the 20th century. These experiences had a profound impact on their values, attitudes, and behaviors. They learned the value of hard work, sacrifice, and frugality, and developed a strong sense of unity and purpose in the face of adversity.

2. Strong Sense of Duty and Patriotism:

The Greatest Generation is known for their strong sense of duty and patriotism. Many of them served in the military during World War II, either by choice or by draft, and were willing to make great sacrifices for their country. They believed in the importance of defending freedom and democracy and were proud to be part of a larger cause.

3. Resilience and Perseverance:

Having lived through the Great
Depression and World War II, the
Greatest Generation developed a
remarkable resilience and ability to
persevere in the face of adversity.
They learned to make do with less,
to be resourceful and self-reliant,
and to keep going even when things
were tough. This resilience has been
a source of inspiration for later
generations.

4. Strong Work Ethic:

The Greatest Generation is known
for their strong work ethic and
dedication to their jobs. They
believed in the value of hard work
and personal responsibility and were
willing to put in long hours to provide
for their families and contribute to
their communities. They took pride in

their work and saw it to build a better future for themselves and their children.

5. Frugality and Thriftiness:

Having grown up during the Great Depression, the Greatest Generation learned the value of frugality and thriftiness. They were careful with their money, avoided waste and extravagance, and believed in saving for a rainy day. They were also resourceful and creative in finding ways to stretch their resources and make the most of what they had.

6. Strong Family Values:

The Greatest Generation placed a high value on family and traditional gender roles. They believed in the importance of marriage, staying together through tough times, and providing a stable home environment for their children. They also tended to have larger families than later generations, with many children born during the post-war baby boom.

7. Respect for Authority and Institutions:

The Greatest Generation had a strong respect for authority and institutions, such as the government, the military, and religious organizations. They believed in the importance of following rules and regulations and trusting in the wisdom and guidance of leaders and experts. They also had a strong sense of community and believed in the importance of contributing to the greater good.

8. Humility and Modesty:

Despite their many achievements and sacrifices, the Greatest Generation is known for their humility and modesty. They did not seek attention or praise for their actions, but rather saw them as a necessary part of their duty and responsibility. They believed in the importance of putting others before themselves and in the value of quiet strength and determination.

The Greatest Generation is a remarkable cohort that has left an indelible mark on American history and culture. Their resilience, work ethic, and dedication to their country have been a source of inspiration for later generations, and their values and experiences continue to shape our society today. As we honor and remember their legacy, it is important to recognize the sacrifices they made and the lessons they can teach us about perseverance, duty, and the power of unity in the face of adversity.

Chapter 3:

The Silent Generation: Born 1928-1945

Born between 1928 and 1945, this generation is often referred to as The Silent Generation. They grew up in a time of economic hardship and political turmoil, facing challenges that shaped their values and beliefs. This generation witnessed the aftermath of World War II and the onset of the Cold War, experiencing uncertainty and instability on a global scale.

The Silent Generation is characterized by their strong work ethic, discipline, and resilience. They value loyalty, duty, and responsibility, traits that were instilled in them from a young age. Growing up during a time of social conformity, this generation learned to adapt to societal expectations and norms, often putting the needs of others before their own. Education played a vital role in the lives of The Silent Generation.

Many of them were the first in their families to pursue higher education, seeking knowledge and skills to secure a better future. Despite limited resources and opportunities, they were determined to succeed and make a difference in the world. The Silent Generation's approach to education was marked by dedication and perseverance. They understood the importance of hard work and self-discipline, values that were instilled in them through their upbringing. With a focus on traditional academic subjects and vocational training, this generation laid the foundation for future generations to thrive and excel. As educators, it is essential to recognize the unique characteristics and experiences of The Silent Generation.

By understanding their values, beliefs, and motivations, we can create learning environments that cater to their needs and preferences. By honoring their contributions and legacy, we can ensure that their impact on education is remembered and celebrated for generations to come.

The Silent Generation, born between 1928 and 1945, played a significant role in shaping the educational landscape of their time. Their values of hard work, discipline, and dedication continue to inspire us today, reminding us of the importance of resilience and perseverance in the face of adversity.

By acknowledging their legacy and honoring their achievements, we can pay tribute to the generation that laid the groundwork for future generations to thrive and succeed.

The Silent Generation, born between 1928 and 1945

The Silent Generation, born between 1928 and 1945, is a unique cohort that has experienced some of the most significant events of the 20th century. They have witnessed the Great Depression, World War II, the Cold War, and the Civil Rights Movement, among other defining moments in history.

These experiences have shaped their values, attitudes, and behaviors in ways that set them apart from other generations.

One of the most distinguishing features of the Silent Generation is their resilience. Growing up during the Great Depression, many members of this generation experienced poverty, scarcity, and economic uncertainty. They watched their parents struggle to make ends meet and learned the value of frugality, saving, and making do with less. This early exposure to hardship instilled in them a strong sense of self-reliance and the ability to adapt to difficult circumstances.

The Silent Generation's formative years were also marked by the turmoil of World War II. While many of their older siblings and parents fought in the war, those on the home front faced rationing, blackouts, and the constant fear of losing loved ones.

They participated in scrap metal drives, planted victory gardens, and supported the war effort in whatever ways they could. This shared experience of sacrifice and unity left a lasting impact on the Silent Generation, fostering a strong sense of patriotism and a commitment to the greater good.

In the post-war years, the Silent Generation came of age in a period of relative prosperity and stability.

The GI Bill provided unprecedented opportunities for education and homeownership, allowing many members of this generation to achieve a middle-class lifestyle.

They entered the workforce during a time of economic growth and stayed with the same company for many years, valuing job security and loyalty over personal fulfillment or entrepreneurship.

This emphasis on stability and conformity is another defining characteristic of the Silent Generation.

They grew up in a time when social norms were more rigid and expectations for behavior were clearly defined. They were taught to respect authority, follow the rules, and not rock the boat. This conformist mindset was reinforced by the specter of the Cold War, which created a culture of suspicion and a fear of being labeled as "un-American."

However, it would be a mistake to paint the Silent Generation as entirely passive or conformist. Many members of this generation played a significant role in the early stages of the Civil Rights Movement, participating in sit-ins, boycotts, and other forms of peaceful protest racial segregation and discrimination. They also challenged traditional gender roles, with more women entering the workforce and pursuing higher education than ever before.

The Silent Generation's political views are often characterized as more conservative than those of subsequent generations. They came of age during the Cold War, when the threat of communism loomed large, and many embraced traditional values and a strong national defense.

However, there is also a streak of pragmatism and moderation in their political beliefs, born out of their experiences of economic hardship and war. They value compromise, cooperation, and incremental progress over radical change or ideological purity.

In terms of family life, the Silent Generation is known for its high marriage rates and low divorce rates. They prioritized family stability and often adhered to traditional gender roles, with men as breadwinners and women as homemakers. As the years passed and social norms began to shift, many Silent Generation women entered the workforce, particularly as their children grew older. They balanced work and family responsibilities in ways that paved the way for future generations of working mothers.

The Silent Generation's contributions to society are often overlooked, but they are no less significant than those of other generations. In politics, notable members of this generation include John F. Kennedy, the first Catholic president, and Sandra Day O'Connor, the first woman to serve on the Supreme Court. In the arts, Silent Generation members such as Harper Lee, author of "To Kill a Mockingbird," and Toni Morrison, Nobel laureate in literature, have left an indelible mark on American culture.

As the Silent Generation enters their later years, they face unique challenges related to aging, healthcare, and retirement. Many are living longer than previous generations, thanks to advances in medical technology and improved living conditions.

However, this also means that they are more likely to experience age-related health issues and to require long-term care. The cost of healthcare and the burden of caregiving often fall on their children and grandchildren, creating new challenges for families and society.

Despite these challenges, the Silent Generation remains a vital and influential presence in society. They offer a wealth of knowledge, experience, and perspective that can inform and guide younger generations. As grandparents and great-grandparents, they play an important role in passing down family history, traditions, and values to future generations. They also serve as a reminder of the importance of resilience, sacrifice, and the greater good in the face of adversity.

In recent years, there has been a growing recognition of the Silent Generation's contributions and experiences. Museums, documentaries, and oral history projects have sought to capture their stories and perspectives before they are lost to time. These efforts are important not only for preserving history but also for fostering intergenerational understanding and appreciation.

As we look to the future, we can learn much from the Silent Generation's example. Their values of hard work, loyalty, and perseverance are as relevant today as they were decades ago. Their commitment to family, community, and country reminds us of the importance of shared sacrifice and the power of unity in the face of adversity.

At the same time, we must also recognize the ways in which their experiences and perspectives differ from those of younger generations and work to bridge the generational divide through open and honest dialogue.

The Silent Generation may be small, but their impact on society is immeasurable. They have witnessed and shaped some of the most significant events of the 20th century and have left a legacy of resilience, determination, and quiet strength that continues to inspire and guide us today.

As we honor their contributions and learn from their experiences, we can build a stronger, more united society for generations to come.

The Silent Generation is a unique and influential cohort that has experienced some of the most defining moments of the 20th century.

Their resilience, conformity, work ethic, and commitment to family and country set them apart from other generations and have left a lasting impact on society.

As they enter their later years, it is more important than ever to recognize and celebrate their contributions, learn from their experiences, and work to build a better future for all. The Silent Generation may be small in number, but their legacy will continue to shape our world for generations to come.

Chapter 4:

Baby Boomers (1946-1964)

Baby Boomers, born between the years 1946 and 1964, represent a significant generation that has left a lasting impact on the field of education.

This cohort, characterized by their sheer numbers and unique experiences, has influenced educational practices, policies, and philosophies in profound ways. One key aspect of the Baby Boomer generation is their strong belief in the value of education.

Growing up in a post-World War II era marked by economic prosperity and increased access to educational opportunities, Baby Boomers placed a high priority on obtaining a good education. This emphasis on learning and knowledge acquisition has shaped the educational landscape for decades to come.

Moreover, Baby Boomers have played a crucial role in shaping the modern education system. As they progressed through their own schooling, many Baby Boomers became educators themselves, bringing their values and perspectives into the classroom.

Their influence can be seen in various educational reforms, curricular changes, and teaching methodologies that have emerged over the years. Furthermore, Baby Boomers have been instrumental in advocating for educational equality and inclusivity.

As a generation that witnessed significant social and cultural transformations, Baby Boomers have championed efforts to provide quality education for all individuals, regardless of background or circumstances. Their commitment to diversity and equity has helped pave the way for a more inclusive educational environment.

Baby Boomers have left an indelible mark on the field of education. Their passion for learning, dedication to improving the educational system, and advocacy for equality have shaped the way we approach teaching and learning today.

As we reflect on the contributions of the Baby Boomer generation, we recognize their enduring legacy in the realm of education.

Baby Boomers, the generation born between 1946 and 1964

Baby Boomers, the generation born between 1946 and 1964, are a unique and influential demographic that has significantly shaped modern society. Born in the aftermath of World War II, they experienced a period of unprecedented economic growth, social change, and technological advancement.

This generation is special and different from others in several ways, including their size, cultural impact, work ethic, and the way they have redefined aging.

Size and Influence:

One of the most notable characteristics of the Baby Boomer generation is its sheer size. The post-war economic boom led to a significant increase in birth rates, resulting in a population surge.

In the United States alone, an estimated 76 million babies were born during this period. This large cohort has had a profound impact on society, shaping everything from consumer trends and popular culture to politics and the economy.

As they entered adulthood, Baby Boomers became a dominant force in the workforce, holding key positions in various industries and driving economic growth. Their collective purchasing power has been unmatched, influencing the development and marketing of products and services. From the rise of suburban living and the popularity of muscle cars in their youth to the growth of the retirement industry as they age, Baby Boomers have been at the forefront of shaping consumer trends.

Cultural and Social Impact:

Baby Boomers came of age during a period of significant cultural and social upheaval. They witnessed and participated in the Civil Rights Movement, the Women's Liberation Movement, the Vietnam War protests, and the counterculture of the 1960s.

These experiences shaped their values, attitudes, and beliefs, making them a generation that challenged the status quo and sought to create a more equitable and just society.

The Boomer generation played a crucial role in advancing civil rights, gender equality, and environmental awareness. They were instrumental in bringing about legislative changes, such as the Civil Rights Act of 1964 and the Environmental Protection Act of 1970. Their activism and idealism laid the foundation for many of the social and political movements that continue to influence society today.

Boomers also had a significant impact on popular culture. They grew up with the rise of rock and roll, Motown, and the British Invasion, which revolutionized the music industry. They witnessed the birth of television and embraced it as a primary source of entertainment and information. The generation's cultural icons, such as the Beatles, Bob Dylan, and Martin Luther King Jr., left an indelible mark on society and continue to inspire subsequent generations.

Work Ethic and Career:

Baby Boomers are known for their strong work ethic and dedication to their careers. Growing up in a time of prosperity and opportunity, they were encouraged to pursue higher education and secure stable, long-term employment. Many Boomers entered the workforce with the expectation of working for the same company for their entire careers, valuing loyalty and job security.

This generation is often associated with the concept of the "workaholic," prioritizing their professional lives and defining themselves through their work. They are known for putting in long hours, climbing the corporate ladder, and striving for success. This strong work ethic has contributed to their reputation as a generation that has driven economic growth and innovation.

However, as Baby Boomers have aged, they have also challenged traditional notions of retirement. Many Boomers are choosing to work beyond the conventional retirement age, either out of financial necessity or a desire to remain active and engaged. They are redefining retirement, with a growing number opting for semi-retirement, entrepreneurship, or second careers later in life.

Technology Adaption:

Although Baby Boomers are not digital natives like younger generations, they have witnessed and adapted to tremendous technological changes throughout their lives. They have seen the rise of television, computers, the internet, and mobile devices, and have had to navigate these advancements in both their personal and professional lives.

While some Boomers may have initially been hesitant to embrace new technologies, many have become adept at using computers, smartphones, and social media.

They have recognized the importance of staying connected and relevant in an increasingly digital world. Baby Boomers have also been a significant driving force behind the growth of industries related to technology, such as personal computers and software development.

However, the rapid pace of technological change has also presented challenges for some Boomers. They may struggle with the constant need to update their skills and adapt to new technologies, particularly in the workplace. This has led to concerns about age discrimination and the need for continuous learning and upskilling throughout their careers.

Redefining Aging:

As Baby Boomers enter their senior years, they are redefining what it means to age. They are challenging traditional stereotypes of aging and embracing the notion of active, engaged, and fulfilling lives in their later years.

Boomers are prioritizing health and wellness, with a focus on maintaining physical fitness, mental acuity, and social connections.

This generation has been at the forefront of the "successful aging" movement, which emphasizes the importance of maintaining independence, purpose, and quality of life as one grows older.

They are seeking out opportunities for lifelong learning, travel, and personal growth, refusing to be defined by their age.

Baby Boomers are also transforming the healthcare and retirement industries. As a large cohort enters their senior years, there is a growing demand for age-related products and services, such as healthcare, assisted living, and leisure activities tailored to their needs and preferences.

This has led to the development of new industries and the adaptation of existing ones to cater to the unique needs and expectations of this influential generation.

Legacy and Challenges:

The Baby Boomer generation has left a lasting impact on society, shaping cultural norms, social movements, and economic trends. Their influence can be seen in the way we work, live, and think about aging. However, as they enter their later years, Boomers also face significant challenges.

One of the primary concerns is the financial security of Baby Boomers in retirement. Many Boomers have not saved enough for their retirement years, and the shift away from traditional pension plans to individual retirement accounts has placed a greater burden on personal financial planning. This has led to concerns about the sustainability of social security and healthcare systems as many Boomers retire.

Another challenge facing Baby Boomers is the changing nature of work and the economy. As industries evolve and automation becomes more prevalent, some Boomers may struggle to adapt to new job requirements or face age discrimination in the workplace.

This has led to discussions about the need for lifelong learning, reskilling, and creating age-friendly work environments.

Additionally, as Baby Boomers age, there is a growing concern about the availability and affordability of healthcare and long-term care services. With longer life expectancies and the prevalence of chronic health conditions, Boomers will require significant healthcare resources in their later years. This has implications for the healthcare system, government policies, and families who may need to provide caregiving support.

Despite these challenges, the Baby Boomer generation remains a resilient and influential force in society. They have demonstrated an ability to adapt to change, innovate, and redefine societal norms throughout their lives.

As they continue to age, they will undoubtedly leave a legacy and shape the future of aging for generations to come.

The Baby Boomer generation is special and different in numerous ways. From their sheer size and economic influence on their cultural impact and redefining of aging.

Boomers have left an indelible mark on society. While they face unique challenges as they enter their later years, their resilience, adaptability, and ongoing contributions to society will continue to shape our world for years to come.

Chapter 5:

Generation X (1965-1980)

GENERATION X, born between 1965 and 1980, is a unique cohort that grew up in a time of significant cultural and technological change. This generation is characterized by their independent, entrepreneurial spirit and their skepticism towards traditional institutions. One of the defining features of Generation X is their adaptability and resilience.

Growing up in a period marked by economic uncertainty and social upheaval, members of this generation learned to navigate challenges and setbacks with a sense of pragmatism and resourcefulness.

This ability to weather storms and bounce back from adversity has shaped their approach to education and career development. In the realm of education,

Generation X values practical skills and hands-on learning experiences. They tend to be more focused on acquiring tangible skills that can be applied in the real world, rather than on theoretical knowledge alone. This generation is known for their DIY mentality and willingness to take on new challenges outside of the traditional academic framework.

Generation X tends to be more individualistic and self-reliant when it comes to their educational pursuits. They are less likely to conform to traditional educational paths and more inclined to seek out alternative routes to learning. This independent streak often translates into a preference for self-directed learning and a willingness to explore unconventional educational opportunities. In the professional sphere, Generation X is marked by their entrepreneurial spirit and desire for autonomy. They are more likely to eschew traditional career paths in favor of forging their own way and pursuing opportunities that align with their personal values and goals.

This generation values work-life balance and seeks out careers that allow them to express their creativity and independence.

Overall, Generation X is a cohort that embodies a spirit of resilience, adaptability, and self-reliance. Their unique approach to education and career development reflects their independent and entrepreneurial mindset, making them a generation that is poised to make a lasting impact on the world around them.

Generation X, born between 1965 and 1980

Generation X, born between 1965 and 1980 is a unique and often misunderstood generation that has made significant contributions to society. Sandwiched between the larger and more well-defined Baby Boomer and Millennial generations,

Gen Xers have often been overshadowed and labeled with stereotypes such as "slackers" or "cynical." However, upon closer examination, Generation X possesses distinctive characteristics, experiences, and values that set them apart and have shaped their impact on the world.

Independent and Self-Reliant:
One of the defining traits of Generation X is their independence and self-reliance. Growing up in a

time of economic uncertainty, political skepticism, and changing family structures, many Gen Xers learned to fend for themselves at an early age. They were the first generation to experience high rates of divorce and dual-income households, leading to the term "latchkey kids" as they often found themselves alone after school.

This early exposure to independence fostered a strong sense of self-sufficiency and adaptability among Gen Xers. They learned to rely on themselves and developed a pragmatic approach to life. This self-reliance has translated into their work ethic and entrepreneurial spirit, with many Gen Xers starting their own businesses or embracing freelance and contract work as a means of maintaining control over their careers and lives.

Bridging the Analog and Digital Worlds:

Generation X is unique in that they straddle the divide between the analog and digital worlds. Born before the widespread adoption of personal computers and the internet, they grew up in a time when technology was rapidly evolving. They witnessed the transition from rotary phones to mobile devices, from typewriters to computers, and from vinyl records to digital music.

This exposure to both analog and digital technologies has given Gen Xers a unique perspective and adaptability. They are comfortable navigating both worlds and have been instrumental in bridging the gap between older and younger generations in the workplace. They understand the value of face-to-face communication and building personal relationships while also embracing the efficiency and connectivity offered by digital tools.

Skepticism and Pragmatism:

Generation X came of age during a time of political and social upheaval. They witnessed the Watergate scandal, the energy crisis, the Cold War, and the AIDS epidemic. They were exposed to the failings of institutions and the limitations of authority figures, leading to a pervasive sense of skepticism and mistrust.

This skepticism has shaped Gen Xers' worldview and approach to life. They tend to question authority, challenge the status quo, and value transparency and authenticity.

They are pragmatic in their decision-making, often seeking practical solutions rather than idealistic outcomes. This pragmatism extends to their approach to work and careers, where they prioritize work-life balance and seek meaningful experiences over blind loyalty to employers.

Entrepreneurial Spirit and Adaptability:

Generation X is known for their entrepreneurial spirit and

adaptability in the face of change. Growing up in an era of economic instability and corporate downsizing, many Gen Xers learned to be resilient and take control of their own destinies.

They have been at the forefront of the entrepreneurial boom, starting businesses and embracing new technologies and industries.

Gen Xers are often described as the "startup generation," with a high percentage of successful entrepreneurs and business leaders belonging to this cohort. They are not afraid to take risks, challenge conventional wisdom, and carve their own paths. This entrepreneurial mindset has also made them adaptable to changing job markets

and willing to reinvent themselves
when necessary.

Work-Life Balance and Family
Dynamics:

Generation X places a high value on
work-life balance and has been
instrumental in shaping modern
workplace culture. Having witnessed
their parents' dedication to work and
the toll it took on family life, many
Gen Xers have sought to prioritize
their personal lives and
relationships.

They have been advocates for
flexible work arrangements,
telecommuting, and family-friendly
policies in the workplace. Gen Xers
understand the importance of finding
a balance between their professional

and personal responsibilities and have been willing to make career sacrifices for the sake of their families.

As parents, Gen Xers have also approached family dynamics differently from previous generations. They tend to be more hands-on and involved in their children's lives, prioritizing quality time and emotional connection. They have also been more open to non-traditional family structures and have been at the forefront of redefining gender roles and expectations within the household.

Cultural Influence and Contributions:

Generation X has made significant contributions to popular culture, art, music, and literature. Growing up in the MTV era, they were exposed to a wide range of musical genres and subcultures. They witnessed the rise of grunge, hip-hop, and alternative rock, and many Gen X artists have left a lasting impact on the music industry.

In film and television, Gen X has been responsible for some of the most influential and iconic works of the past few decades. Directors such as Quentin Tarantino, Christopher Nolan, and Wes Anderson have redefined cinema with their unique storytelling and visual styles. Gen X writers and producers have also been at the forefront of the prestige television revolution, creating groundbreaking series that have pushed the boundaries of the medium.

Gen Xers have also made significant contributions to literature, with authors such as David Foster Wallace, Bret Easton Ellis, and Jhumpa Lahiri producing works that capture the zeitgeist of their generation. They have explored themes of alienation, consumerism, and the search for meaning in a postmodern world, offering insights into the Gen X experience.

Technology and Digital Pioneers: Generation X has played a crucial role in the development and adoption of digital technologies. Many of the key figures behind the rise of the internet, social media, and e-commerce belong to this generation. Gen Xers were early adopters of personal computers, online communities, and mobile devices, and they have been instrumental in shaping the digital landscape.

Gen X entrepreneurs and innovators have founded some of the most influential technology companies of the past few decades. From the creation of Google and Amazon to the development of smartphones and apps, Gen Xers have been at the forefront of the digital revolution. They have also been leaders in fields such as cybersecurity, data analytics, and artificial intelligence, driving technological advancements that have transformed industries and society.

Political and Social Activism:
While often characterized as apathetic or disengaged, Generation X has made significant contributions to political and social activism. They have been involved in movements such as environmentalism, LGBTQ+ rights, and racial justice, using their skepticism and pragmatism to challenge systemic inequalities and push for change.

Gen Xers have been leaders in grassroots organizing, leveraging digital tools and social media to mobilize communities and raise awareness about important issues. They have also been active in local politics, running for office and advocating for policies that reflect their values and priorities.

As they have entered positions of power and influence, Gen Xers have brought their unique perspectives and experiences to bear on political and social discourse. They have been champions of diversity, inclusion, and social responsibility, pushing for greater representation and equity in various spheres of society.

Legacy and Future Impact:

As Generation X enters midlife and assumes leadership roles in various fields, their impact on society continues to grow. They are shaping the future of work, technology, politics, and culture, bringing their independence, adaptability, and pragmatism to bear on the challenges of the 21st century.

Gen Xers are poised to play a critical role in addressing pressing issues such as climate change, income inequality, and the rapid pace of technological change. Their entrepreneurial spirit and innovative thinking will be essential in developing solutions and driving progress.

As they age, Gen Xers are also redefining what it means to grow older in a rapidly changing world. They are challenging traditional notions of retirement and aging, embracing lifelong learning, and seeking out new experiences and opportunities well into their later years.

The legacy of Generation X will be one of resilience, adaptability, and quiet revolution. While often overshadowed by the larger generations that bookend them, Gen Xers have made an indelible mark on society through their unique perspectives, contributions, and values. As they continue to shape the world around them, their impact will be felt for generations to come.

Generation X is a special and different generation that has defied stereotypes and made significant contributions to society. From their independence and entrepreneurial spirit to their bridging of the analog and digital worlds, Gen Xers have brought a unique set of skills, values, and experiences to bear on the challenges and opportunities of their time. As they continue to lead and innovate in various fields, their impact will undoubtedly shape the future in profound and lasting ways.

Chapter 6:

Millennials/(1981-1996)

Millennials, also known as Generation Y, born between 1981 and 1996, are a unique cohort that has been shaped by the technological advancements and societal changes of their time. This generation is often characterized by their affinity for digital technology, their strong sense of social justice, and their desire for work-life balance. One of the key aspects of Millennials is their upbringing in a period of rapid technological growth. Unlike previous generations, Millennials grew up in a world where the internet was readily accessible, leading to an unprecedented level of connectivity and information at their fingertips. This has influenced not only how Millennials communicate and interact with others but also how they approach learning and education. In the realm of education,

Millennials have shown a preference for collaborative and interactive learning environments. They value hands-on experiences and practical applications of knowledge rather than rote memorization. This shift in learning styles has led to changes in traditional educational practices, with an increased emphasis on project-based learning, group work, and technology integration in the classroom.

Millennials are driven by a strong sense of social responsibility and a desire to make a positive impact on the world. This generation is more likely to prioritize social causes and environmental sustainability in their personal and professional lives. As such, they seek educational experiences that align with their values and provide opportunities for them to effect change in society. Additionally, Millennials value work-life balance and seek careers that offer flexibility and fulfillment.

They are more likely to prioritize personal well-being and meaningful work over traditional markers of success such as salary or status. This attitude towards work has influenced their approach to education, with Millennials seeking out programs and institutions that support their holistic development and well-being.

Millennials, or Generation Y, represent a generation that is reshaping education with their tech-savvy, socially conscious, and work-life balance-oriented mindset. Educators and institutions must adapt to the needs and preferences of this generation to provide them with the best possible learning experiences and prepare them for success in an ever-changing world.

**Millennials, also known as
Generation Y**

Millennials, also known as
Generation Y are the demographic
cohort born between 1981 and 1996.
This generation has grown up in a
world vastly different from that of
their predecessors, shaped by rapid
technological advancements,
globalization, and significant social
and economic changes.

Millennials possess unique
characteristics, values, and
experiences that set them apart from
previous generations, making them
a force to be reckoned with in
various aspects of society.

Digital Natives:

One of the defining characteristics of Millennials is their status as digital natives. Born into a world where computers, the internet, and mobile devices were rapidly becoming ubiquitous, Millennials have grown up with technology as an integral part of their lives. They are the first generation to have had access to the internet from a young age, and they have embraced digital communication, social media, and online platforms as natural extensions of their social lives and personal identities.

This deep familiarity with technology has shaped the way Millennials communicate, learn, work, and interact with the world around them.

They are adept at navigating digital landscapes, quickly adapting to new technologies, and leveraging online resources for personal and professional growth. This digital proficiency has also influenced their expectations and preferences, with Millennials seeking out seamless, intuitive, and connected experiences in all aspects of their lives.

Diversity and Inclusion:

Millennials are the most diverse generation in history, with a significant proportion identifying as racial or ethnic minorities. They have grown up in a world where diversity and inclusion have been central themes in public discourse, and they have been exposed to a wide range of cultures, perspectives, and experiences from a young age.

This exposure has shaped Millennials' attitudes towards diversity and inclusion, with many embracing these values as fundamental to their worldview. They are more accepting of differences, more open to diverse perspectives, and more committed to creating inclusive environments in their personal and professional lives.

Millennials have been at the forefront of movements promoting social justice, equality, and representation, using their collective voice and influence to drive change.

Entrepreneurial and Collaborative:

Millennials have a strong entrepreneurial spirit and a collaborative approach to work and problem-solving. Growing up in an era of rapid change and economic uncertainty, many Millennials have rejected traditional career paths in favor of creating their own opportunities.

They are more likely than previous generations to start their own businesses, pursue freelance or gig work, or seek out roles that align with their values and passions.

At the same time, Millennials value collaboration and teamwork. They recognize the power of collective intelligence and the importance of diverse perspectives in driving innovation and success. Millennials thrive in environments that foster open communication, knowledge sharing, and cross-functional collaboration. They are comfortable working in teams, both in-person and virtually, and they value the sense of community and purpose that comes from working towards common goals.

Socially Conscious and Value-Driven:
Millennials are a socially conscious generation, deeply concerned about issues such as climate change, social justice, and economic inequality. They have grown up in a world where these challenges have been at the forefront of public discourse, and they feel a strong sense of responsibility to make a

positive impact on society and the planet.

This social consciousness has shaped Millennials' values and priorities, both in their personal lives and in their professional pursuits. They seek out companies and organizations that align with their values and prioritize corporate social responsibility, environmental sustainability, and ethical business practices.

Millennials are more likely to support brands and causes that reflect their beliefs, and they are willing to use their purchasing power and influence to drive change.

Work-Life Integration and Flexibility:

Millennials have a different approach to work-life balance than previous generations. Rather than striving for a strict separation between their personal and professional lives, they seek work-life integration and flexibility. They value the ability to blend their work and personal commitments, and they prioritize employers and roles that offer the flexibility to do so.

This desire for flexibility has been driven in part by the changing nature of work, with technology enabling remote work and 24/7 connectivity. Millennials have embraced these changes, recognizing the potential for greater autonomy, productivity, and work-life harmony. They are more likely to seek out roles that offer flexible schedules, remote work options, and the ability to pursue personal interests and passions alongside their professional commitments.

Lifelong Learning and Personal Growth:

Millennials place a high value on lifelong learning and personal growth. They recognize that in a rapidly changing world, continuous skill development and adaptation are essential for success and fulfillment. Millennials are more likely than previous generations to prioritize ongoing education, whether through formal programs, online courses, or self-directed learning.

This focus on personal growth extends beyond the acquisition of technical skills. Millennials also prioritize soft skills, such as emotional intelligence, communication, and leadership, recognizing their importance in navigating complex social and professional landscapes. They seek out experiences and opportunities that allow them to grow as individuals, both personally and professionally, and they are willing to invest time and resources in their own development.

Digital Content Creators and Influencers:

Millennials have been at the forefront of the rise of digital content creation and influencer culture. Growing up with social media and online platforms, they have recognized the power of these tools to express themselves, build communities, and influence others. Many Millennials have become content creators, bloggers, vloggers, and social media influencers, leveraging their skills and personalities to build personal brands and engage with audiences around the world.

This shift towards user-generated content and influencer marketing has disrupted traditional media and advertising models, with Millennials playing a significant role in shaping the new media landscape. They have also been early adopters of emerging platforms and technologies, such as podcasting, live streaming, and virtual reality, constantly pushing the boundaries of what is possible in the digital realm.

Political and Civic Engagement:

Millennials are a politically engaged generation, with a strong sense of civic responsibility and a desire to shape the world around them. They have grown up in a time of significant political and social upheaval, and they have been exposed to a wide range of perspectives and movements through social media and online platforms.

This exposure has fueled Millennials' activism and involvement in political and social causes. They are more likely than previous generations to participate in protests, sign petitions, and engage in online activism. They are also more likely to prioritize issues such as climate change, racial justice, and LGBTQ+ rights in their political choices and actions.

At the same time, Millennials have a complex relationship with traditional political institutions and processes. They are more likely to identify as independents rather than aligning with a particular political party, and they are often skeptical of established power structures and systems. This has led to a desire for political reform and a willingness to support unconventional candidates and movements that challenge the status quo.

Delayed Life Milestones and Changing Family Structures:

Millennials have experienced significant shifts in the timing and nature of key life milestones, such as marriage, parenthood, and homeownership. Compared to previous generations, Millennials are getting married later, having children later, and are more likely to live with their parents or in shared housing arrangements.

These shifts have been driven by a range of factors, including economic uncertainty, changing social norms, and a desire for personal and professional flexibility.

Millennials prioritize experiences and personal growth over traditional markers of adulthood, and they are more open to alternative family structures and living arrangements.

At the same time, Millennials who do choose to marry and have children are approaching these roles differently than previous generations. They are more likely to prioritize equal partnerships, shared parenting responsibilities, and work-life integration in their family lives. They are also more open to non-traditional family structures, such as same-sex marriages and single parenthood.

Mental Health and Wellness:

Millennials have grown up in a world where mental health and wellness have become increasingly important topics of conversation and concern.

They are more likely than previous generations to openly discuss mental health challenges, seek out support and resources, and prioritize self-care and emotional well-being.

This focus on mental health and wellness has been driven in part by the unique stressors and challenges faced by Millennials, such as economic uncertainty, student debt, and the constant pressure to succeed in a fast-paced, always-connected world.

Millennials have been at the forefront of efforts to destigmatize mental health issues, promote wellness practices, and create more supportive and inclusive environments in their personal and professional lives.

Millennials are a unique and influential generation, shaped by the rapid technological, social, and economic changes of their time. As digital natives, they have embraced technology as a central part of their lives, using it to connect, create, and drive change. They are a diverse and inclusive generation, committed to social justice, equality, and representation in all aspects of society.

Millennials are also entrepreneurial and collaborative, seeking out opportunities to create their own paths and work together towards common goals. They are socially conscious and value-driven, using their influence and purchasing power to support causes and brands that align with their beliefs. They prioritize work-life integration, flexibility, and personal growth, and they are willing to invest in their own development and well-being.

As content creators, influencers, and political activists, Millennials are shaping the media landscape and driving social and political change. They are navigating new family structures and life milestones, and they are prioritizing mental health and wellness in a world that can be stressful and overwhelming.

As Millennials continue to age and assume leadership roles in various aspects of society, their unique perspectives, skills, and values will undoubtedly shape the future in profound and lasting ways. They are a generation poised to make a significant impact on the world, and their influence will be felt for generations to come.

Chapter 7:

Generation Z or iGen (1997-2012)

GENERATION Z Or IGEN (1997-2012) In this chapter, we delve into the unique characteristics and traits of Generation Z, also known as iGen, born between the years 1997 and 2012.

This generation has grown up in a world vastly different from that of their predecessors, facing challenges and opportunities shaped by rapid technological advancements and shifting cultural landscapes. One defining feature of Generation Z is their deep immersion in the digital realm. From a young age, members of this generation have been surrounded by smartphones, social media platforms, and instant access to information.

This constant connectivity has not only shaped their communication styles but also influenced their perceptions of the world around them. Despite being labeled as digital natives, Generation Z is also characterized by a strong sense of social awareness and activism.

This generation is passionate about issues such as climate change, social justice, and equality, using their online platforms to raise awareness and advocate for change. Their desire to make a positive impact on society sets them apart as a generation driven by purpose and authenticity. Moreover,

Generation Z displays a remarkable aptitude for multitasking and adaptability. Growing up in an era of rapid change and innovation, members of this generation have learned to navigate complex environments with ease, often juggling multiple responsibilities simultaneously.

This ability to pivot and embrace new challenges positions Generation Z as a cohort poised to thrive in an ever-evolving world.

As educators, understanding the unique characteristics of Generation Z is crucial in effectively engaging with and supporting this generation of learners.

By harnessing their digital fluency, social consciousness, and adaptability, educators can create learning environments that resonate with the values and preferences of Generation Z, fostering a sense of belonging and empowerment.

In the following chapters, we will explore strategies and best practices for engaging Generation Z students in the classroom, leveraging their strengths to create meaningful learning experiences and prepare them for success in an increasingly digital and interconnected world. Join us as we embark on a journey to uncover the potential and promise of Generation Z, a generation poised to shape the future with their unique blend of innovation, empathy, and resilience.

Generation Z, also known as iGen or Centennials

Generation Z, also known as iGen or Centennials, is the demographic cohort succeeding Millennials, born between 1997 and 2012. This generation has grown up in a world shaped by rapid technological advancements, social media, and significant global events, making them a unique and influential group. In this 2000-word analysis, we will explore the key characteristics, values, and experiences that set Generation Z apart from previous generations.

1. Digital Natives:

Generation Z is the first generation to be born into a world where the internet and digital technology are ubiquitous. They have grown up with smartphones, social media, and constant connectivity as an integral part of their lives. This immersion in technology from a young age has had a profound impact on the way they communicate, learn, and interact with the world around them.

Gen Zers are adept at navigating digital platforms, multitasking across devices, and processing vast amounts of information quickly. They are comfortable with rapidly evolving technologies and are quick to adapt to new digital tools and platforms. This digital fluency has also influenced their social interactions, with a significant portion of their relationships and communication taking place online.

2. Social Media and Online Identity:

Social media plays a central role in the lives of Generation Z. They have grown up with platforms like Facebook, Instagram, Snapchat, and TikTok, using them to express themselves, build communities, and stay connected with friends and family. For Gen Zers, their online presence is an extension of their identity, and they are skilled at curating their digital persona to reflect their values, interests, and aspirations.

However, this constant connectivity and exposure to social media has also had its challenges. Generation Z is more likely to experience issues such as cyberbullying, online harassment, and the pressure to maintain a perfect online image. They are also more aware of the impact of their digital footprint and are cautious about the information they share online.

3. Diversity and Inclusivity:

Generation Z is the most diverse generation in history, with a significant proportion identifying as racial or ethnic minorities, LGBTQ+, or gender non-conforming. They have grown up in a world where diversity and inclusion have been central themes in public discourse, and they have been exposed to a wide range of cultures, perspectives, and experiences from a young age.

Gen Zers value diversity and inclusion as fundamental principles, and they are more likely to actively advocate for social justice and equality. They expect the brands, organizations, and leaders they support to align with their values and take meaningful action towards creating a more inclusive and equitable society. They are also more comfortable with fluid and multifaceted identities, rejecting rigid labels and categories.

4. Mental Health and Wellness: Generation Z has grown up in a world where mental health and wellness have become increasingly important topics of conversation and concern. They are more likely than previous generations to openly discuss mental health challenges, seek out support and resources, and prioritize self-care and emotional well-being.

This focus on mental health has been driven in part by the unique stressors and challenges faced by Gen Zers, such as the constant pressure to succeed in a fast-paced, always-connected world, the impact of social media on self-esteem and relationships, and the uncertainty of the future in the face of global crises like climate change and economic instability.

5. Entrepreneurial and Creative:

Generation Z has a strong entrepreneurial spirit and a desire to create their own opportunities. They have grown up witnessing the rise of young entrepreneurs, influencers, and content creators who have built successful careers and businesses through digital platforms. This has inspired many Gen Zers to pursue their own entrepreneurial ventures, whether through starting online businesses, developing apps, or creating digital content.

Moreover, Gen Zers are highly creative and value self-expression. They are comfortable with using digital tools and platforms to showcase their talents, whether through art, music, writing, or video. They are also more likely to pursue creative careers or incorporate creativity into their work, seeing it to make a meaningful impact and express their unique perspectives.

6. Pragmatic and Financially Conscious:

Generation Z has grown up in the shadow of significant global events, such as the Great Recession, climate change, and political uncertainty. This has made them a pragmatic and financially conscious generation, aware of the challenges they face and the importance of being prepared for the future.

Gen Zers are more likely to prioritize financial stability and security, seeking out practical skills and education that will help them succeed in an increasingly competitive job market. They are also more cautious about debt and are more likely to save money and seek out cost-effective solutions in their personal and professional lives.

7. Activism and Social Responsibility:

Generation Z is a socially conscious and politically engaged generation.

They have grown up in a world where social and environmental issues have been at the forefront of public discourse, and they feel a strong sense of responsibility to make a positive impact on the world.

Gen Zers are more likely to participate in activism, whether through online campaigns, protests, or volunteering. They are passionate about issues such as climate change, racial justice, LGBTQ+ rights, and gender equality, and they use their collective voice and influence to drive change and hold those in power accountable.

8. Education and Learning:

Generation Z has a unique perspective on education and

learning. They have grown up in a world where information is readily available at their fingertips, and they are comfortable with self-directed learning and seeking out knowledge on their own.

However, they also recognize the value of formal education and are more likely to pursue higher education than previous generations.

They are interested in educational experiences that are interactive, collaborative, and relevant to their interests and career goals. They also value diversity and inclusion in education and are more likely to seek out schools and programs that reflect their values.

9. Authenticity and Transparency:

Generation Z values authenticity and transparency in their personal and professional relationships. They have grown up in a world where information is easily accessible and where deception can be quickly uncovered, making them highly attuned to insincerity or inconsistency.

Gen Zers are more likely to gravitate towards brands, influencers, and public figures who are genuine, honest, and transparent about their values and actions. They are quick to call out hypocrisy or inauthenticity and are more likely to support companies and individuals who align with their values and demonstrate a commitment to social responsibility.

10. Global Awareness and Connectivity:

Generation Z has grown up in a globally connected world, with instant access to information and perspectives from around the globe. They are more aware of global issues and are more likely to have friends and connections across borders.

This global awareness has influenced their values and perspectives, making them more open to diverse cultures and experiences. They are also more likely to see themselves as global citizens, with a responsibility to address challenges that transcend national boundaries, such as climate

change, inequality, and human
rights.

Generation Z is a unique and
influential generation that is poised
to shape the future in significant
ways. Their immersion in digital
technology, commitment to diversity
and inclusion, entrepreneurial spirit,
and social consciousness set them
apart from previous generations.

As they enter adulthood and begin to
take on leadership roles in various
fields, their perspectives and values
will undoubtedly drive significant
changes in the way we live, work,
and interact with one another. They
are a generation that is not afraid to
challenge the status quo, embrace
creativity and innovation, and work

towards a more just and sustainable world.

However, Generation Z also faces unique challenges, such as the impact of social media on mental health, the uncertainty of the future in the face of global crises, and the pressure to succeed in an increasingly competitive world. As a society, it is crucial that we support and empower this generation, providing them with the resources, opportunities, and guidance they need to thrive and make a positive impact on the world.

As we look to the future, Generation Z will play a pivotal role in shaping the world we live in. Their unique perspectives, skills, and values will be essential in addressing the complex challenges and opportunities of the 21st century, from climate change and social justice to technological innovation and global collaboration.

By understanding and embracing the strengths and challenges of Generation Z, we can work together to create a more inclusive, sustainable, and equitable world for all.

Chapter 8:

Generation Alpha (2013-2024)

Generation Alpha (2013-2024) is a unique cohort born between 2013 and 2024, characterized by their innate connection to technology and their diverse perspectives on global issues.

This generation has grown up in a world where information is constantly at their fingertips, shaping their views on education and learning in unprecedented ways.

One of the defining features of Alpha Generation is their digital fluency. From a young age, they are exposed to smartphones, tablets, and other devices that have become integral parts of their daily lives. This early exposure has not only accelerated their technological skills but has also influenced the way they absorb and process information.

Education in the Alpha Generation must adapt to meet the needs of these tech-savvy individuals. Traditional methods of teaching are no longer sufficient to engage this generation of learners. Educators must embrace technology as a tool for enhancing learning experiences and promoting critical thinking skills. Interactive platforms, online resources, and collaborative projects can all be utilized to create a dynamic and engaging educational environment for Alpha Generation students.

Furthermore, the Alpha Generation is growing up in a world that is increasingly interconnected. Global issues such as climate change, social justice, and technological advancements are shaping their understanding of the world around them. Educators must incorporate these topics into the curriculum to foster a sense of global citizenship and empathy among Alpha Generation students.

As we navigate the educational landscape of the Alpha Generation, it is essential to recognize the unique characteristics and needs of these young learners. By harnessing their digital fluency, embracing technology in education, and addressing global issues in the curriculum, educators can empower Alpha Generation students to become informed, critical thinkers who are prepared to tackle the challenges of the 21st century.

Generation Alpha, born between 2013 and 2024

Generation Alpha, born between 2013 and 2024 is the youngest generation in our society today. As the children of Millennials, they are growing up in a world that is vastly different from any previous generation. This generation is set to be the most technologically advanced, globally connected, and demographically diverse generation yet. In this 2000-word exploration, we will delve into the unique characteristics, influences, and potential future impact of Generation Alpha.

1. Born into a Digital World:

Generation Alpha is the first generation to be born entirely within the 21st century, and they are growing up in a world where technology is seamlessly integrated into every aspect of their lives. From the moment they are born, they are surrounded by smartphones, tablets, and smart home devices. This constant exposure to technology is shaping the way they learn, communicate, and interact with the world around them.

Unlike previous generations, Generation Alpha will not know a world without the internet, social media, or artificial intelligence. They will be natural adopters of new technologies and will expect technology to be intuitive, responsive, and personalized to their needs. This innate digital literacy will have a profound impact on their education, careers, and personal lives, as they navigate a world where technology is constantly evolving.

2. Artificial Intelligence and Automation:

Generation Alpha will grow up in a world where artificial intelligence (AI) and automation are increasingly prevalent. They will be the first generation to have AI as a constant companion, from personalized educational software to virtual assistants and self-driving cars. This exposure to AI will shape their expectations and interactions with technology, as they come to rely on intelligent systems to navigate their daily lives.

The impact of AI and automation on the workforce will also be significant for Generation Alpha. As machines take over many routine and manual tasks, this generation will need to develop skills that are uniquely human, such as creativity, critical thinking, and emotional intelligence. They will also need to be adaptable and open to continuous learning, as the pace of technological change accelerates, and new jobs emerge while others become obsolete.

3. Globalization and Cultural Diversity:

Generation Alpha is being born into a world that is more globally connected than ever before. With the proliferation of the internet and social media, they will have instant access to information and perspectives from around the globe. This exposure to diverse cultures, languages, and ways of life will shape their worldview and make them more open-minded and accepting of differences.

As global mobility continues to increase, Generation Alpha will also be more likely to have friends, family, and colleagues from different parts of the world. They will be comfortable navigating multicultural environments and will value diversity as a key strength in their personal and professional lives. This global mindset will be essential as they tackle complex challenges that transcend national borders, such as climate change, public health crises, and economic inequality.

4. Environmental Awareness and Sustainability:

Generation Alpha will inherit a planet that is grappling with the consequences of climate change, pollution, and environmental degradation. From a young age, they will be exposed to the urgency of these issues and will grow up with a deep understanding of the need for sustainable practices and environmental stewardship.

This generation will be more likely to prioritize sustainability in their personal choices, from the products they buy to the careers they pursue. They will also be more likely to hold businesses and governments accountable for their environmental impact and will expect them to take meaningful action to address climate change and protect natural resources.

5. Mental Health and Well-being:

As the children of Millennials, who have been vocal about the importance of mental health and self-care, Generation Alpha will grow up with a greater awareness of the need to prioritize their well-being. They will be more likely to openly discuss mental health challenges and seek out support when needed.

However, Generation Alpha will also face unique stressors and challenges, such as the constant pressure to curate a perfect online persona, the impact of social media on self-esteem and relationships, and the uncertainty of growing up in a world that is rapidly changing. As a result, there will likely be a greater emphasis on developing resilience, emotional intelligence, and coping skills from a young age.

6. Personalized and Lifelong Learning:

Generation Alpha will have access to an unprecedented amount of information and educational resources from a young age. They will be able to learn at their own pace and pursue their interests through online courses, educational apps, and virtual reality experiences. This personalized approach to learning will allow them to develop skills and knowledge that are tailored to their individual strengths and goals.

However, the rapid pace of technological change will also mean that the skills and knowledge that Generation Alpha learns in school may become quickly outdated. As a result, lifelong learning will be essential for this generation to stay relevant and adapt to new challenges and opportunities.

They will need to be comfortable with continuous upskilling and reskilling throughout their careers and will value educational experiences that are flexible, practical, and relevant to their changing needs.

7. Entrepreneurship and Innovation: Growing up in a world where technology has lowered the barriers to entry for starting a business, Generation Alpha will be more entrepreneurial and innovative than previous generations. They will have access to tools and platforms that allow them to turn their ideas into reality, whether it's creating a new app, starting an e-commerce

business, or launching a social enterprise.

This entrepreneurial spirit will be fueled by Generation Alpha's creativity, digital literacy, and desire to make a positive impact on the world. They will be more likely to pursue unconventional career paths and create their own opportunities, rather than relying on traditional employment models. As a result, we may see a proliferation of new businesses, products, and services that are created by and for Generation Alpha.

8. Social Justice and Equity:

Generation Alpha will grow up in a world where social justice and equity are central issues. They will be exposed to movements such as Black Lives Matter, #MeToo, and the fight for LGBTQ+ rights from a young age and will be more likely to actively advocate for inclusion and equality.

This generation will expect the brands, organizations, and leaders they support to take a stand on social issues and will be more likely to hold them accountable for their actions and impact on marginalized communities. They will also be more likely to seek out diverse and inclusive environments in their personal and professional lives and will value organizations that prioritize equity and belonging.

9. Blurred Boundaries and Work-Life Integration:

For Generation Alpha, the boundaries between work and life will be increasingly blurred. They will grow up in a world where remote work and flexible work arrangements are the norm, and where technology allows them to stay connected and productive from anywhere.

As a result, this generation will value work-life integration and will expect their employers to support their holistic well-being. They will be more likely to prioritize experiences and personal fulfillment over traditional markers of success, such as salary and job title. They will also be more open to non-linear career paths and may have multiple careers or pursuits over the course of their lives.

10. Adaptability and Resilience:

Growing up in a world that is constantly changing, Generation Alpha will need to be highly adaptable and resilient. They will face challenges and disruptions that are unprecedented in scale and complexity, from climate change and economic uncertainty to technological disruption and social unrest.

To thrive in this context, Generation Alpha will need to develop strong problem-solving skills, emotional intelligence, and the ability to navigate ambiguity and change. They will also need to be open to new ideas and perspectives and will value collaboration and teamwork as essential skills for success.

Generation Alpha is poised to be a transformative force in the world, shaped by a unique set of influences and experiences. As the first generation to grow up entirely in the 21st century, they will be at the forefront of technological, social, and environmental change.

Their innate digital literacy, global mindset, and entrepreneurial spirit will allow them to create new solutions and opportunities that we can't yet imagine. At the same time, they will face significant challenges, from the impact of climate change and economic inequality to the need for lifelong learning and mental health support.

As a society, we have a responsibility to support and empower Generation Alpha, providing them with the resources, skills, and opportunities they need to thrive in a rapidly changing world. By understanding and embracing their unique strengths and challenges, we can work together to create a more just, sustainable, and equitable future for all.

The impact of Generation Alpha will be felt for decades to come, as they take on leadership roles in business, government, and civil society. Their values, perspectives, and actions will shape the course of the 21st century and beyond, and it is up to all of us to ensure that they have the support and guidance they need to

fulfill their potential and make a
positive impact on the world.

Chapter 9:

The study of different generations.

Characteristics, values, and
experiences can provide valuable
insights into societal trends,
consumer behavior, workforce
dynamics, and cultural shifts. By
understanding the unique
perspectives and needs of each

generation, we can work towards creating a more inclusive, equitable, and prosperous society. Here are some ways we can use this information to progress:

1. Fostering Intergenerational Collaboration:

By recognizing the strengths and challenges of each generation, we can promote intergenerational collaboration and knowledge sharing. For example, Baby Boomers and Generation X can share their experience and wisdom with younger generations, while Millennials and Generation Z can bring fresh perspectives and digital skills to the table. By creating opportunities for intergenerational dialogue and collaboration, we can foster innovation, creativity, and problem-solving.

2. Adapting Education and Workforce Development:

As each generation enters the workforce with different skills, expectations, and learning styles, educational institutions and employers need to adapt to meet their needs. This may involve creating more flexible and personalized learning experiences, providing opportunities for continuous learning and upskilling, and creating inclusive and diverse work environments that value the contributions of all generations.

3. Addressing Generational Inequities:

By understanding the unique challenges and opportunities faced by each generation, we can work towards addressing generational inequities and creating a more level playing field. For example, we can address the student debt crisis that disproportionately affects Millennials, or the digital divide that may limit access to opportunities for older generations. By creating targeted policies and programs that address the needs of each generation, we can promote greater social and economic mobility.

4. Embracing Diversity and Inclusion:

Each generation brings a unique set of experiences, values, and perspectives to the table, and this diversity can be a powerful asset for organizations and society. By embracing and celebrating the diversity of each generation, we can create more inclusive and equitable environments that value the contributions of all individuals, regardless of age or background.

5. Designing Products and Services:

Understanding the unique needs, preferences, and behaviors of each generation can help businesses and organizations design products and services that meet the needs of a diverse range of consumers. For example, by understanding the digital preferences of Generation Z and Alpha, businesses can create more engaging and personalized digital experiences.

By understanding the health and wellness needs of Baby Boomers, healthcare providers can create more targeted and effective interventions.

6. Promoting Civic Engagement and Social Change:

Each generation has the potential to drive social and political change, and by understanding their unique perspectives and priorities, we can create more effective and inclusive movements for progress. For example, by harnessing the activism and social consciousness of Millennials and Generation Z, we can create more powerful campaigns for climate action, racial justice, and gender equity.

7. Planning for the Future:

By understanding the long-term implications of generational shifts, we can plan and create more sustainable and resilient societies. For example, by understanding the aging population of Baby Boomers, we can create more effective policies and programs for healthcare, retirement, and social security. By understanding the environmental concerns of Generation Alpha, we can create more ambitious plans for climate action and sustainability.

The study of different generations provides a powerful lens for understanding the complexities and opportunities of our changing world. By embracing the unique strengths and challenges of each generation, and working towards greater intergenerational collaboration and understanding, we can create a more inclusive, equitable, and prosperous future for all.

Chapter 10:

What will history tell us about each generation?

What will history tell us about each generation? Each generation leaves behind a unique legacy that shapes the course of history. From the Baby Boomers who witnessed significant social change to Gen Xers who embraced technology, each generation has made its mark on the world.

The Baby Boomers, born after World War II, are remembered for their activism and push for civil rights and gender equality. They challenged the status quo and paved the way for future generations to continue the fight for justice and equality.

Generation X, born between the early 1960s and early 1980s, grew up during a time of rapid technological advancement. They were the first to embrace computers and the internet, setting the stage for the digital age we live in today. Gen Xers are known for their independence and resilience in the face of economic challenges.

Millennials, born between the early 1980s and mid-1990s, are often characterized as tech-savvy and socially conscious. They are the generation that grew up with the internet and social media, using these platforms to advocate for change and connect with others on a global scale.

Generation Z, born in the late 1990s and early 2000s, are true digital natives. They have never known a world without smartphones and social media. Gen Z is known for their creativity, diversity, and commitment to social justice causes.

As we look back on each generation, we can see how their unique experiences and values have shaped the world we live in today. From fighting for civil rights to embracing technology, each generation has made its mark on history in its own way.

What will history tell us about the generations to come? Only time will reveal the legacy they leave behind. Thank You for reading. I hope you found this eBook interesting. Please look at some of my other books available at all book retailers and online.